Surviving The Waiting Room

By: Jacqueline Roberts

Surviving the Waiting Room
by Jacqueline Roberts
(c)2003

First Printing: September 2003

Cover Design by Stacey W. Fontenot

All Scripture quotations in this book are from the King James Version of the Bible unless otherwise identified.

All rights reserved. No portion of this publication may be reproduced, stored in an electronic system, or transmitted in any form or by any means, electronic, mechanical, photocopy, recording, or otherwise, without the prior permission of Jacqueline Roberts. Brief quotations may be used in literary reviews.

Printed in United States of America by
Fontenot's Business Forms
613 Alamo Street
Lake Charles, LA
337.436.0814

Library Of Congress Catalog Card Number
ISBN 0-9745989-0-9

Dedication

I have chosen to dedicate this book to my sister, Paula Johnson, who waited for many years in the waiting room and is now beginning to walk through the door into her destiny.

Contents

Acknowledgments iii

Introduction v

Chapter One - The Timing of God 1

Chapter Two - Mankind Comes on the Scene 7

Chapter Three - The Promised Isaac 9

Chapter Four - The Widow's Needs are Met 13

Chapter Five - Menial Task or Miracle Act 15

Chapter Six - One Preserved Dream .17

Chapter Seven - Willing to do My Part 21

Chapter Eight - Second Chances 25

Chapter Nine - Unlikely Resources .27

Chapter Ten - The Right Place at the Right Time 31

Chapter Eleven - Controlling Your Emotions 33

Chapter Twelve - The Love of God .39

Chapter Thirteen - Condemnation or Conviction 45

Chapter Fourteen - Submission = Blessing 49

Chapter Fifteen - Into Your Destiny 53

Acknowledgments

First and foremost, I want to give honor to Jesus Christ for allowing me to be the vessel He chose to flow through to give this message to those who need encouragement while awaiting their destiny.

I want to give honor to my husband for releasing me to minister as the Lord moves upon me.

I want to give honor to my parents, Robert and Nancy Stirnemann for being the best examples of loyal and faithful Christians that I could have had.

I want to give honor to our "Bishop" who has impacted our lives and ministry more than any other human being that has touched our lives.

I want to give honor to Bro. W. L. Sciscoe for reading my book and encouraging the publishing of it.

I want to thank my two beautiful children, Jocelyn and Kaleb for being patient as mommy finished taking care of business.

Thank you to Stacey Fontenot for all your help on this project.

Introduction

One of the most frustrating places for a child of God to be in is the waiting room. You know what God has promised. You know where He wants to take you in life. You are well aware of the ministry He has called you to. However, you do not *see* anything happening. Bottled up anointing is like lit dynamite inside a container that does not allow it to explode.

This book is about having a promise from God that has not come to fruition yet, the interim period. The way we respond in this time period will determine our outcome.

I pray that you will feel encouraged and challenged as you read this book. Learn the lessons you come across in the waiting room. Try not to look at your situation as a prison. Remember God specializes in *Divine Delays*.

The Timing of God

CHAPTER ONE

The Word of God says, "...with His stripes we are healed", (Isaiah 53:5) but you haven't received your healing yet. The Word of God says, "A man's gift maketh room for him, and bringeth him before great men," (Proverbs 18:16) but there does not appear to be any room for your gift. The Word of God says, "Lo, children are an heritage of the Lord: and the fruit of the womb is his reward", (Psalms 127:3) but still you have no child. The Word of God says, "But my God shall supply all your need according to his riches in glory by Christ Jesus", (Philippians

4:19) but you do not see how your bills are going to get paid. Somebody prophesied over you regarding your future and nothing has happened yet. You've been called to preach but *nobody's called you.*

These are very frustrating situations to be in. Sometimes we find ourselves questioning whether the Word of God really means what it says. **Yes it does!** I am sure you have heard it preached numerous times that God's timing is not our timing and to everything there is a season.

Well, I had heard it all. I was beginning to loathe the waiting room when God spoke something to my heart that I had never heard before. He said, "Do you just want out of your prison or do you want to walk into your destiny?" It hit me like a ton of bricks. I had felt like a caged lion but after God spoke to me, I felt a calm come upon me.

Many times in trying to encourage people to wait on the timing of the Lord we will refer to

Joseph as an example. God gave Joseph dreams at a young age of his future as a ruler over his parents and siblings. Yet instead of ruling over them, his siblings threw him into a pit and then he was sold into slavery. While in Potiphar's house, Joseph begins to move up the ladder and possibly begins to feel as though this will be the way God has chosen to bring his dreams to pass by making him a ruler on the job. And before he realizes what has happened he is falsely accused by Potiphar's wife of making advances toward her and he winds up in prison. Hopes smashed. Dreams dead. Once again, Joseph begins to see a flicker of hope as he moves up the chain of command in the prison. Joseph *always* excelled at whatever situation he found himself in, even in prison. What a break when the butler and baker of the king are cast into prison and need a dream interpreter. Joseph interprets their dreams and asks the butler to remember him before the king when he is restored to bearing the king's cup. Joseph wants out of his prison! However, the butler forgets him and does not remember Joseph for two years. Some of us would have allowed hatred to creep in toward the butler. Many times we think people have control over our destiny, however, **they don't!** God has *all* power. He did not allow the butler to remember Joseph at that time. "The king's heart is in the hand of the Lord...he turneth it whithersoever he will" (Proverbs 21:1). Why did God make Joseph wait two more years? God's perfect timing.

The timing of the Lord is indeed way beyond our comprehension. We say, "Why not now God?" We say, "I think this is the best time for that promise Lord." "I'm ready Lord." "Did you hear me God? I'm ready." Then there are times when we begin to question if we really heard from God at all. Was I *really* called to preach? Did God *really* give me the singing voice I have to use for His glory? Maybe it is the will of God for me to stay sick. Maybe I am cursed and do not deserve to have a child.

I want to remind you of some instances in the Word of God where timing was *everything*.

Jacqueline Roberts

Mankind Comes on the Scene

CHAPTER TWO

Y ou may wonder why God chose to create mankind on the sixth day. Then again, maybe you have never thought about it. If God would have made Adam on the first day, what a disaster that would have been. Adam would have died of starvation, dehydration, lack of oxygen or froze to death. Mankind could not exist if created sooner than the sixth day. He certainly would not have enjoyed his surroundings as much. No trees, no flowers, no beautiful running brooks, no sun, moon and stars. Just think about it, God knew when the right time was for mankind to come on the scene.

We must remember that truly *all* things do work together for our good. God prepared the environment to introduce his most treasured creation, mankind. After each step was taken, God *"saw that it was good."* Many times God is setting the stage in our lives to bring us into the place that He has foreordained us to be in.

The Promised Isaac
CHAPTER THREE

I'm reminded of Abraham and Sarah. Abraham had directly heard the voice of God telling him he would be a father of many nations. Now, why in the world did God make them wait so long? God *always* has a reason for the timing He chooses. I think He made them wait so long for many reasons. One was so that everybody would know that Isaac's conception and birth were an absolute miracle. I believe another reason was to test Abraham's faith. And last but not least, I believe the reason God made them wait so long to have Isaac was because of what was going on in the world at the time. If they had begged and pleaded with God to have Isaac much earlier, Isaac would have never married whom he was supposed to marry. Therefore, the lineage of Jesus Christ would have been altered.

You may say, "Well I don't believe it matters to God who a person marries." I beg to differ. When Abraham sent his eldest servant to find a wife for Isaac the servant prayed, "...that the damsel to whom I shall say, Let down thy pitcher, I pray thee, that I may drink; and she shall say, Drink, and I will give thy camels drink also: let the same be she that thou hast appointed for thy servant Isaac;" (Genesis 24:14). If it didn't matter who would mother Isaac's children, why did it matter who mothered Isaac? God did *not* allow Hagar to mother Isaac. Sarah was the one chosen to give him birth. Rebekah was the chosen one to give birth to Jacob whom the bloodline of Jesus Christ would pass through. God chooses to use *who* He wants *when* He wants and if we will be willing and obedient to His plan things will happen in their appointed time.

Jacqueline Roberts

The Widow's Needs are Met

CHAPTER FOUR

Let's take a look at the widow of Zarephath in I Kings chapter 17. God told Elijah to go to Zarephath and he would find a widow woman there to sustain him. The widow woman had basically *nothing* in her house, only enough meal and oil to make her and her son a cake. She was at the point of hopelessness. Elijah said, "Make me thereof a little cake first...and after make for thee and for thy son. For thus saith the Lord God of Israel, The barrel of meal shall not waste, neither shall the cruse of oil fail, until the day that the Lord sendeth rain upon the earth"

(I Kings 17:13-14). The woman was *obedient*. She had enough *faith* to believe the man of God.

Sometimes we are in the waiting room because we still need to learn another lesson before God can trust us with such a great blessing as the widow woman received. Many times, it is just another act of obedience He is waiting on. Possibly God is testing you to see if you *really* have put your trust in Him. "Trust in the Lord, and do good; so shalt thou dwell in the land, and verily thou shalt be fed" (Psalms 37:3). The widow never again had to worry about feeding her and her son.

Menial Task or Miracle Act?
CHAPTER FIVE

Often we are still in the waiting room because of our own stubbornness. Naaman was a leper who came to Elisha the prophet to receive his healing. (II Kings 5) Naaman was a proud man we can assume because of his response to the instruction he was given by the man of God. Elisha told Naaman to go wash in the river Jordan seven times and he would be clean. Naaman did not like these instructions and the Bible says he went away *wroth*. He was angry. Sometimes God will test our spirit by allowing us to be asked to do something that we feel is beneath us or is menial. Remember the Word of God tells us to deny *self*, take up our cross, and follow Jesus. The river Jordan was a filthy body of water. Why couldn't Elisha have told him to go wash in the rivers of Damascus, which were better?

Naaman did get his miracle when he finally subjected himself to the filthy waters of Jordan in obedience. Were the waters what healed him? No. It was his willingness and obedience to do that which was asked of him.

One Preserved Dream

CHAPTER SIX

Some of you are in the waiting room waiting on the Lord to remove a hindrance or an obstacle from your path so you can go on and do the will of God. You may have had somebody try to destroy you. Possibly they succeeded at killing some of your dreams. Remember, God is able to resurrect the dead. If the dream was God-given, nobody can stop the dream from happening except *you*.

Athaliah was the mother of king Ahaziah. (II Kings) She was a *wicked* woman. When her son, the king, died she had all the seed royal destroyed, her own grandchildren, so that she could reign as queen. That is...she *thought* she destroyed all the seed royal.

There are times when it may seem that people are getting away with what they have done to you but God has the last say so. The most important thing we can do when those types of situations happen in our lives is to forgive the person and release them into the hands of God. "...Vengeance is mine; I will repay, saith the Lord" (Romans 12:19). Bitterness will keep you from walking in to your destiny.

I had gone through an extremely painful ordeal and told God that I just did not have the strength to forgive this person for what they had done to me. God spoke back to me and said, "What did I pray on the cross?" I said, "You know Lord that verse has always bothered me, '...Father, forgive them; for they know not what they do' (Luke 23:34), that's always been a hard one to explain to people who do not believe you are One." God spoke back to me and said, "I couldn't forgive what they had done to me in my flesh either, I had to cry out to the divinity within me to forgive." Whoa! Total revelation! I began praying, "Lord, I forgive and where my flesh is incapable of forgiving I ask You to forgive through me." "I can do all things through Christ which strengtheneth me" (Philippians 4:13).

Jesus was not asking His daddy to forgive what someone had done to him. His flesh was dependent upon the Spirit within Him. If you have received the gift of the Holy Ghost, you have that same Spirit within you to forgive.

When the one remaining seed royal who had been hid during the massacre was seven years old, God chose to bring him into his season, into his rightful position and spare the nation of Judah further abuse by Athaliah.

Athaliah was put to death at the word of Jehoiada the priest. I imagine the people of Judah thought all their hope was dead but God had one "dream" preserved. One "dream" that He would bring into being in His time. However, the people of Judah had to endure Athaliah until Joash was "old enough" to sit on the throne.

Willing to do My Part

CHAPTER SEVEN

We're familiar with the story of Esther. Esther's destiny came to fruition when somebody else disobeyed the king. If queen Vashti would have never disobeyed her husband, king Ahasuerus, Esther would have never taken her rightful place as the queen and been in that favored position at the right time.

God saw to it that Esther would be chosen as the succeeding queen. Esther did her part. She kept herself looking good and was willing to go through the purification process and do whatever it took to become the next Mrs. Ahasuerus.

We too need to be willing to go through the purification process. And have the attitude of "whatever it takes."

People are deceived who are not willing to do their part in making their destiny happen.

I'm reminded of a story I heard a pastor tell about one of his female relatives who cried on his shoulder because she did not have a husband. He asked her what kind of man she wanted and she proceeded to tell him. He responded to her by telling her that she *really* did *not* want the kind of man she had just described. She emphatically declared, "Yes, I do". He said, "If you really want the kind of man you just described you would lose weight and learn how to cook and serve". She did just that and within a short amount of time she was engaged to be married to the kind of man she wanted.

Sometimes we want to spiritualize things too much and not look at the practical side of things.

God chose Esther to be queen at the appointed time so that she could spare her people, the Jews, from being put to death by Haman. (Esther)

Jacqueline Roberts

Second Chances
CHAPTER EIGHT

Some have already had their name called while in the waiting room but did not like the door they were asked to walk through.

Jonah's name was called but he did not want to go where God wanted him to go. Nineveh was wicked. Jonah chose to run the other way. However, God kept calling him. If Jonah had lived in this day and age and was seen as running from his call some would have written him off.

Many of you may have run from your call or your destiny but still God is calling. Maybe you feel that you have been "written off". Jonah had his second chance and so do you. You may have to wind up in the "belly of a great fish" before you decide to answer the call of God. You may have to get to the point where you realize that everything around you *stinks* before you give in to the voice of the Lord. We can only imagine what it felt and smelled like to be in the belly of that great fish.

Jonah prayed unto the Lord out of the fish's belly and said, "I cried by reason of mine affliction unto the Lord, and he heard me; out of the belly of hell cried I, and thou heardest my voice" (Jonah 2:2). Jonah walked into his destiny and an entire city repented. You have no idea what may happen if you walk through the door that has been opened to you.

Unlikely Resources

CHAPTER NINE

When it was time to pay tribute in Matthew chapter 17, neither Jesus nor His disciples had the money to pay. Jesus told Peter, "...go thou to the sea, and cast an hook, and take up the fish that first cometh up; and when thou hast opened his mouth, thou shalt find a piece of money: that take, and give unto them for me and thee" (Matthew 17:27). You may feel like you are drowning in a sea of debt. Grab onto the life preserver that God has thrown out to you. He said He would supply *all* of our needs, not wants, but needs. He has the ability to cause a financial miracle to come your way from the most unlikely of resources. Put your trust in Him. Your miracle is not far off.

We were renting a house down south when the real estate agent contacted us. She wanted to know if we could move out one month early because our landlord was having financial difficulties and needed to move into his rental. I said, "Sure." As it was, our finances had tightened up a bit and we needed to move some place cheaper. She said, "I hope you didn't give the landlord a deposit because you probably won't get it back." We had given a nine hundred dollar deposit.

A few days went by and I was weeping before the Lord and prayed, "Lord you know we need that money, we are Your children, I would do *anything* for my children." God spoke back to me and said, "Are you *capable* of loving your kids more than I love you?" My faith was nil. There was a knock at the door and my landlord came in and asked me if we had given him a deposit. I told him we had. He reached into his pocket, pulled out a wad of one hundred dollar bills, and handed me our deposit. I was very thankful that in spite of my lack of faith God heard my cry. God *always* comes through on time.

Jacqueline Roberts

The Right Place at the Right Time

CHAPTER TEN

The greatest destiny recorded in the Word of God was that of Jesus Christ. Everything had to line up exactly right for Him to come on the scene. All the prophesies concerning Him had to line up perfectly. He *had* to be born of a virgin. Joseph was warned to move Mary and Jesus from Bethlehem to Egypt to escape Herod who was seeking to kill the new born king, that the scripture might be fulfilled, "Out of Egypt have I called my son" (Matthew 2:15). Joseph was warned again to move his family to Nazareth in order to stay clear of Herod's son, Archelaus, that the word of the prophets, "He shall be called a Nazarene" (Matthew 2:23) might be fulfilled.

At this present time, my husband and I have moved our family to six different states in approximately fifteen years. Sometimes I have asked myself, why? Unfortunately, there are no scriptures that foretell our future as was told of our Saviour. However, when you are led by the Spirit of God you may find yourself very mobile for a time in your life. You may not be able to see the "why?" now, but when you reach your final destiny you will understand. Everything boils down to being at the right place at the right time.

Controlling Your Emotions
CHAPTER ELEVEN

Many emotions can engulf a person while they are waiting on the timing of the Lord. At times it may seem as though you are on an emotional roller coaster. Something good happens and you get your hopes up. Then something discouraging happens and your emotions plummet downward.

I have ridden this roller coaster many times in my life. It is not an enjoyable ride such as those at an amusement park. That is why we **must** walk by faith and not by sight. Walk by faith and *not* by feeling.

I remember one of the most discouraging times in my life was when my husband and I felt that we were on our way to exactly where God was calling us. In the midst of all the wonderful things that were going on, those who had been helping us grow in our ministry rejected us. "He is despised and rejected of men; a man of sorrows, and acquainted with grief." (Isaiah 53:3) Jesus knew exactly how I felt. I had to force myself to be oblivious to the feelings that tried to overwhelm me. Force myself not to act upon my emotions. Force myself to believe that God *did* have an appointed place picked out for us to walk into.

Whenever devastating things would occur, I always had something deep down inside telling me that in spite of what was happening *now* God still had a plan. After one of these disheartening times, to my utter horror, that "something" deep down inside was no longer there. All my hope was dead. I felt as though I was having a nervous breakdown. I knew I had two precious children that God had given me to nurture and here I was caving in to my emotions. I had to get hold of the horns of the altar and the loins of my mind and not allow those feelings to destroy me.

Feelings come from your thought life. If we dwell on things, our emotions follow. If you have been unjustly treated and begin to rehash the scenario over and over again you will feel hatred, rejection, hopelessness. We *must* guard our minds.

God does have your best interest at heart. "For I know the thoughts that I think toward you, saith the Lord, thoughts of peace, and not of evil, to give you an expected end" (Jeremiah 29:11).

Emotions *can* be a positive thing. Jesus was moved with compassion. Compassion is a feeling for someone else's sorrow that leads you to help them. The Bible says He is "touched with the feeling of our infirmities;"(Hebrews 4:15).

Having gone through much pain in your life can cause you to be sensitive to someone else's pain, to cause you to reach out and help them. "Rejoice with them that do rejoice, and weep with them that weep" (Romans 12:15).

I was excited when a minister prophesied over me that I would be ministering to hurting women. I knew I had already gone through many painful ordeals in my life and had been speaking at ladies meetings. However, I did not realize exactly *what* all I would have to go through in order to be more effective in ministering to hurting women. It has been quite a rough road but I made it through. And you will make it through as well. We know where our help comes from.

When emotions try to overtake you while you are waiting on God, bring the emotions in line with the Word of God. Do not allow thoughts of hopelessness to conquer you. The enemy would love to stop you before you make it to your appointed place at the appointed time.

There are times when a thought contrary to

the Word of God will go through my mind and I have learned to say aloud, "I refuse that thought because it is against the Word of God." The Word is a sword and we need to memorize verses that we can speak aloud to destroy the onslaught of the enemy of our destiny and soul. There is truly power in the spoken Word.

If you have allowed that something inside of you to die, remember, our God raises the dead. Let that flicker of hope be rekindled in your spirit. You've got Jesus on your side.

Jacqueline Roberts

The Love of God
CHAPTER TWELVE

When we come to the *revelation*, not realization, that our God *really* does love us, nothing will be able to detour us from the path to our destiny. Some people have the head knowledge that God loves them but they do not have the heart and spirit knowledge of His love.

A preacher once told me that people, especially women, view God the same way they viewed the important males in their life. I began to think about what he had said and was totally amazed how exactly right he was. The pastor that

I had most of my life was a powerfully anointed man of God and I loved him very much. However, he scared me to death! It seemed as though I could do no right in his eyes.

This was exactly the way I viewed my Lord. I felt that even with all my trying, I could never be good enough.

I knew when I first started singing in church at the age of eight I had felt the anointing of God. I felt I was to marry a minister since I was a teen. I knew I wanted to please God above everything else but it seemed impossible for me. I thought to myself, "I am not good enough so God will not use me."

After this minister enlightened me regarding my perception of God, I had to change my thinking. I had to begin reading the Bible all over again. This time there were no preconceived ideas. I took everything I read exactly the way it was written. The love of God became so incredibly real to me.

God had begun waking me up at 1:30 am to pray. I grew to love His wooing. He would call me and I would respond.

One night, about a year later, God was still waking me at 1:30 am to pray. This night would be different though. I got out of bed and went to the living room to pray. I expected that I would start interceding like usual but the tongues did not come.

I began to love on the Lord and He began to reciprocate that love. This went on for about an hour when all of a sudden a word came before my face. J-E-D-I-D-I-A-H. I thought this to be a little strange because it had never happened before. The word kept flashing and I determined I would have to check my concordance to see if it really was a word. It seemed that if it really were a word it would be Biblical.

As I ran my finger down the page of my concordance, I came across the word Jediah. I knew that was not the word I saw in prayer. A little further down was the word Jedidah. This was a little closer to Jedidiah but my feeling was if Jedidiah was not in there than it was just a figment of my imagination. As I continued down the page my heart was pounding hard and there I saw it, J e d i d i a h. It is in one verse in the Bible, II Samuel 12:25. I read the verse and then the chapter and then decided to look in the margin where the definition was. Jedidiah: Beloved of the Lord. I began to weep profusely. I was so amazed that God wanted to speak His love to me and did so in "secret code".

We truly are His beloved. When we come to this revelation our waiting will be more endurable.

"The Lord hath appeared of old unto me, saying, Yea, I have loved thee with an everlasting love: therefore with lovingkindness have I drawn thee" (Jeremiah 31:3).

I personally believe that one of the tactics of the enemy is to cause us to lose faith in the love of

God. It is easy to put complete trust in someone who you know has your best interest at heart. There are going to be times when we just need to pick up the Word of God, read it, and *make* ourselves believe what it says. Like the words of the old song ...*Oh love of God how rich and pure, how **measureless** and strong, it shall forevermore endure...*

When the rough times come, we must be convinced that God *does* love us and He must have a good reason for what is going on right now.

We know that Love *does* the right thing. I remember as a child when my father made the decision to get rid of our television. He told us that he was bothered by some of the things they had started showing on it and thought it was in the best interest of us kids to get rid of it. My two older siblings did not seem bothered at all by dad's decision but my brother who is two and a half years older than me and

I were a *little* upset. Dad's love for us had won out and caused him to do the right thing.

God's love for us causes Him to do the right thing for us as well. We might not think so in the midst of our circumstances but hindsight will prove it true.

Where you are currently may not be the place you desire to be in but God has a reason. He knows what is best for you. His love always wins out. He does the *right* thing.

I remember when my pastor was preaching one time he made the statement, "You have got to trust God enough that even if He chooses to take one of your children at a young age, you accept His will. He knows if your child would have grown up and walked away from Him. Eternity is all that matters."

Condemnation or Conviction

CHAPTER THIRTEEN

I heard one of our great preachers preach a message when I was in Bible College years ago entitled, "Condemnation, the Besetting Sin of Pentecost."

Sometimes I think we do not know how to differentiate between condemnation and conviction. Condemnation will just cause you to feel guilt and unloved and you may not even know what you are feeling that way about. Condemnation will cause you to want to run from God. Conviction, on the other hand, will cause you to feel bad about something in particular and cause you to want to run toward the mercy of God.

Condemnation cripples and torments a person. Conviction frees a person once they act upon it.

I had many regrets for years over a failure in my life. I had truly repented but was continually tormented in my mind. I was talking with my pastor one night and telling him how I felt. A couple nights later at church he pulled me to the front of the altar and said, "I was in prayer about your situation and God told me He does not even know what you are talking about." I was set free that night from condemnation.

We know that satan is the accuser of the brethren. If you are doing wrong conviction will cause you to repent and get right. God will not turn you away when you come to Him in a spirit of repentance.

I believe many have left the waiting room *and the building* because of condemnation. I would like to invite you back into the building, back into the waiting room. God is not finished with you yet. None of us will ever be worthy. You cannot erase your past. However, you can step back onto the path to your destiny. God is still waiting on you. Your destiny is still there.

If you have had an anointing on your life, rest assured that God has plans for you. The anointing breaks the yolk. We need more anointed children of God in this day and age to break the yolk of bondage that our nation is in. People who know how to let God flow through them. People who know how to connect with their Maker.

Remember, we are aware of the enemy's devices. Condemnation is one of them. You have the more powerful weapon. The Word of God.

Jacqueline Roberts

CHAPTER FOURTEEN
Submission = Blessing

Submission. In order to make it to your destiny you must make sure that you are in submission to whomever God has set over you. Submission is not just an act of obedience. Submission is obedience with a willing spirit. "If ye be willing and obedient, ye shall eat the good of the land" (Isaiah 1:19).

We know that God has set up an umbrella of protection for those who are willing to submit to it. We submit to God, our pastors, our husbands, employers and so on. Whoever has been put over you as an authority figure is who you are to submit to.

There is tremendous blessing accompanied with a submissive spirit.

I remember shortly after having learned what *true* submission was I had my first test. It seemed more like a final exam. My husband and I had a disagreement and I left the room. I went into another bedroom and began to pray. God spoke to me and said, "Go to Brian and kneel before him. Wrap your arms around his legs and tell him you submit to him and ask him to lay hands on your head and pray for you." You may ask how I knew this was the voice of God. Well, I definitely knew it was not the enemy and I definitely knew my flesh did not want to do this. I obeyed God and did as He told me with a broken spirit.

A few days later at church our pastor came to my husband and asked him what happened. Pastor said he felt in the Spirit that something significant had taken place in our marriage. It is amazing what will happen when we submit to the voice of God.

I remember the story that one of our ministers has told regarding his own life. He said as a young man he had began to evangelize and line up all kinds of meetings. In the middle of a hopping revival, his pastor called and told him to come home. Because of this man's great spirit, he obeyed and came home. The pastor made him cancel all his meetings and sit for one year. At the end of that one year, the pastor gave the young evangelist a brand new car and his blessing to go and do the work of God. This young evangelist is now a well known preacher among us.

You may feel that you are being mistreated or wronged. I want to remind you that your God has all power. When you choose to truly submit to the Word of God great things will follow. They may not happen overnight or as quickly as we would like to see them happen. However, having God's blessing upon your life is of utmost importance.

The young evangelist could have taken matters into his own hands. He could have said, "Forget it, God is using me, you don't know what you're talking about." However, look what happened when Sarah took matters into her own hands. We got Ishmael.

Submit yourself to the timing of God. I know it is rough. I have been down that road.

Into Your Destiny
CHAPTER FIFTEEN

You may feel as though your circumstances are a prison to you. I did. However, the rest of what God spoke to me regarding "out of your prison or into your destiny" was this; Joseph's destiny, the position which God had appointed for him, ***did not even exist*** until two years after Joseph had interpreted the dreams of the butler and baker. Had Joseph gotten out of prison *when he wanted out* he would have missed his destiny. He would have had to settle for less than God had planned for his life. God intended for him to rule and rule he did.

Because God let him out of his prison at the right time.

We are always brought into our destiny to help others. This may not sound true to those of you who have battled infertility or an illness. However, when your waiting time is over you will have a testimony that will help someone else. A couple in the church I was raised in had been married for 18 years before God gave them a child. The husband gladly told *everyone everywhere* he went about their miracle baby.

The preparation period that you have gone through to walk into your ministerial destination will cause you to be all the more effective for the Kingdom of God. Keep believing. Keep preparing. Keep being consistent. Your waiting time is just about over.